This edition published 2007 by Concordia Publishing House
3558 S. Jefferson Avenue, St. Louis, MO 63118-3968
1-800-325-3040 • www.cph.org

Text © 1988 Concordia Publishing House

Illustrations © 2007 by Concordia Publishing House

Manufactured in China

1 2 3 4 5 6 7 8 9 10   16 15 14 13 12 11 10 09 08 07

The Visit of the Wise Men

Martha Jander

with

Illustrations by Lin Wang

CONCORDIA PUBLISHING HOUSE • SAINT LOUIS

Long ago and far away
some thinkers—very wise—
Each evening watched the sun go down;
they watched the starry skies.

They knew the moon; they knew each star;
they studied planets too.
The Wise Men drew their charts and maps;
their wisdom grew and grew.

One night as darkness dimmed the light

and stars began to shine,

Appeared a brand new star to them—

a star so big and fine.

The Wise Men knew a special joy;

they shouted out, "Prepare!

This star can only mean one thing:

a King is born! But where?"

They left their homes to find that King;
they carried gifts of love.
The star shone brightly on their way,
a brilliant guide above.

'Twas Jesus whom they rightly sought;
 'twas Herod whom they found —
The king of all Jerusalem,
 the meanest man around.

The Wise Men asked King Herod, "Where,

oh, where's this newborn King?

We want to worship Him with love,

to Him our praises sing."

But wicked Herod couldn't say
where Jesus had been born.
He did not know, he could not tell
what happened Christmas morn.

So Herod told his scholars, "You
must look for all you're worth
In ev'ry book and scroll to learn
this place of kingly birth."

They answered, "Yes! In Bethlehem,
King David's family town—
That must be where this Babe lives now."
(King Herod hid his frown.)

That awful king paced back and forth;

he was a jealous man!

"Another king will take my crown,"

he thought. Then he made a plan:

"Please go and find this King," he said,
"then hurry back and say
Exactly where He lives so I
can worship Him some day."

King Herod's very wicked heart
had blurted out this lie.
He'd never worship Jesus Christ;
he wanted Him to die!

The Wise Men left Jerusalem

to go to Bethlehem,

And in the darkened sky they saw

the star, still guiding them.

So they rejoiced with happy hearts;

with hope they traveled fast

Until they saw the star stand still.

They'd found the Child at last!

In front of Jesus, bowing down,

they praised their Savior-Lord.

With gifts of gold and frankincense

and myrrh, He was adored.

Then in a dream that night they heard
the voice of God say, "Go!
Go back home another way,
but not to Herod! No!"

The Wise Men did what God had said,
though Herod's anger grew.
For Jesus, Savior, Son of God,
had godly work to do.

You see, this Babe was born to be
our perfect, sinless Lord,
Who would give His life for all,
and who is by all adored.